May Briganria's
waters flow in
your favour ☺

BRIGANTIA: SONGS OF THE EXALTED

HYMNS TO BRIGANTIA, THE CELTIC MINERVA OF IRON-AGE BRITAIN

NICO SOLHEIM-DAVIDSON &
MURIEL MERSER

First Printing: 2025

Printed by lulu.com
ISBN 978-1-326-72140-4

Facebook.com/NorthSeaPoet
Instagram.com/NorthSeaPoet
ko-fi.com/NorthSeaPoet
threads.com/@NorthSeaPoet

Instagram.com/murielmerser
Threads.com/@murielmerser

Introduction
Written by Nico Solheim-Davidson

Several years ago, this book wouldn't have even been a thought to cross my mind. Or at least as a collaboration it wouldn't have crossed my mind, since I'm not one for collaborations as such. I had since late 2022 an early 2023 been wanting to write something that would be aimed more at the Brittonic Polytheist community, whether it was a "Hymn Book" (Similar to Verses of the Nine Worlds) or a general book of rituals and prayers or something like that. So when I read some of Muriel Merser's poetry, I immediately asked her if she wanted to write a devotional book to Brigantia with me. Fortunately, she said yes, otherwise this book would be half the size it is now.

But who is Brigantia? There isn't enough space in these pages to go in-depth as to who Brigantia is, so I'll try to keep it brief. Brigantia was likely the tutelary deity of the Brigantes, a Celtic tribe in North England whose territory covered most of Yorkshire, as well as most of North England and Southern Scotland. To the Romans, Brigantia was similar enough to goddesses such as Fortuna, Victoria, Minerva, and Tanit that in the few archaeological finds relating to her show her as having imagery associated with Minerva, Fortuna, Victoria or taking on names that either shows her as being syncretised with deities such as Tanit, and Victoria. Looking beyond Brigantia in Britain, it is believed that the goddess survived in Irish traditions, becoming Brigid —the names are certainly etymologically linked but I, personally, am of the belief that the goddess turned saint Brigid and the goddess Brigantia are two separate and distinct beings —and there is evidence to suggest Brigantia was worshipped in the mainland of Europe, in regions such as Gaul, as the goddess Brigandu. But beyond archaeological finds, there is not much we know of the goddess, Brigantia.

This book, to use Muriel's words, is a mixture of "archaeologically-sound praise poems that are in a sense a direct form of communion with Brigantia", and "distorted gestures at a mythology we don't have". As me and Muriel are both devotees or worshippers of Brigantia, this has become what I feel is a beautiful devotional work to Brigantia, and hopefully something that will help anyone that's exploring Brittonic Polytheism, and in particular Brigantia.

My own poems in this book mix my own UPG (unverified personal gnosis) with the epithets found for Brigantia in the handful of Roman inscriptions dedicated to her. Muriel, on the other hand, mixes storytelling into her poems in this book. But I have prattled on enough about the book now, so I will let you enjoy the book in peace without further word spilling from myself about it.

Dêva katâ pâlin kane
mâ eðði avillos tove
kon skamâbos tangvâtique
kon anatlâi avelâique
dedar Brigantias Noibas
svesin Bardâbos kentubos
kanete Naturîganias
svî îsarnî in tankobos.

Sing, skilled goddess,
If it is your will,
may the winds of inspiration
light upon your tongue
shape a song of holy Brigantia,
first of the bards,
the Poet-Queen,
she of the ironwrought peace.

ACKNOWLEDGEMENTS

Special thanks to Drunertos, for whose work in the Brittonic Polytheism community made this book possible.

Hestia   1

First Hymn to Brigantia   2

Aphrodite   3

Hymn to Brigantia the Nymph   5

Athena   6

Hymn to Victoria Brigantia   7

Ogmios   8

Hymn to Celestial Brigantia   10

Maponos   11

Hymn to Tutela Brigantia Augusta   13

Cathubodua   14

Sixth Hymn to Brigantia   15

Brixtâ   16

Seventh Hymn to Brigantia   18

Epona   19

Hymn to Brigantia of the Flames   21

Andraste   23

Ninth Hymn To Brigantia   27

Mnemosyne   28

Hymn to Brigantia of Winter's Beck   29

Hera   30

Hymn to Brigantia Lugrînâ   31

Sirona   32

Hestia

Written by Muriel Merser

Her breath is the balm of the wind
her hand is the red hand of dawn
her tongue is the hammer of song
that shapes symphonies from bleak din

The names of the others have dimmed
nigh all but their effigies gone
her breath is the balm of the wind
her hand is the red hand of dawn

Cathedrals rose over her well
to silence the earth and the sky
and yet in the rushes, her sign
recalls the old songs of her kin
her breath is the balm of the wind.

First Hymn to Brigantia

Written by Nico Solheim-Davidson

I sing to you, O Brigantia,

Fearsome queen, crowned with turrets

Exalted upon hill and mountain

And greeted over river and stream

O High One, Throned atop the Pennines

Guardian of the Northward Lands

From Humber to Hadrian's Wall

I sing to you, in your triumphant glory

O Brigantia, awe-inspiring goddess

You, Fierce Heart of Yorkshire,

Bordered by mountain and sea

I sing to you now and shall again

Aphrodite

Written by Muriel Merser

The way to Asphodel was made dark
so that mortals cannot see the other side
the lantern of Mnemosyne
reflects upon the waters of the Lethe
the shades' only memory
is the familiar old face
that time will take as her prize.

I am called Merciful
When I raise my hand o'er the painted sky
where once I shared the name of Hera
Lightbearing Morning-Star,
Queen of Heaven

I am called Laughter-Loving
there under the mountain
where pomegranate seeds take root
where Tannhäuser kneels
at the foot of my throne
my many guests drink and glory.

And I am called Warlike.
My husband envies me my smithy,
where I forge the steel
that my lover and I wield in battle.
I am the Sky-Daughter
born of the foaming waves of the sea
I am Queen in the Hollow Mountain
and the sovereign of all passions.

Hymn to Brigantia the Nymph

Written by Nico Solheim-Davidson

O Brigantia, Nymph of Northern Rivers
You who bring waters of life and healing
And delight in the flowing streams
I sing to you, in your aqueous glory

Nymph and Water-Draped Queen
You who flows through Dale and Moor
And rejoices throughout Wold and Meadow
As to sea and ocean you flow

Nymph and Goddess of Northern Waters
O Brigantia, crowned in streams, I sing to you
From your waters, sacred and wild, grant to me
Favour throughout the seasons where you flow

Athena

Written by Muriel Merser

A roman made a statue of me
crowned like a rampart, clad in green
spear in my right hand, orb in my left,
Medusa's locket upon my breast,

he called me by your name
and you answered with my voice
now we are one
and your stories shall be my stories
and your nature shall be my nature

Strangers from an unnamed land are we,
the moon and the moon's half-sisters three
she leads the dead o'er the dancing sky
my aegis raised, I hold the line

I am she of measured boldness
who needs no tricks to have my way
to protect what must be protected
by salve or by steel.

Hymn to Victoria Brigantia

Written by Nico Solheim-Davidson

O Brigantia, winged victory
Fearless warrior, armed with spear
And with wreath in hand

O Brigantia, triumph bringer
The one who makes peace
And grants us victory

O Brigantia, driver of war-chariot
Who stands upon the world
With palm-branch in hand

O Brigantia, victory goddess
Wielder of spear and wreath
I sing to you and shall again

Ogmios

Written by Muriel Merser

OGMIOS:

"Brixtâ, seek you Brigantiâ

the daughter of Taranis

whom Epona loves well

companion of invincible Andraste

taught the cures by almighty Sirona

taught at the forge by stout Gobannos

taught poetry by Nantosuelta of the Honeyed Fields

who loves mortals and is beloved by them

she has freed those who were bound to me

bound by the chains Gobannos forged for me."

BRIXTÂ:

"All have learned from Sirona

who coils within and without

Gobannos has also taught many

and all who feel love know Nantosuelta.

I cannot seek her by Taranis' name

for fatherhood is but a claim

only the name of her mother

may guide my hexing hand.

And who is that, Ogmios?

Who bore Brigantiâ?

Was it Epona? Nantosuelta? Cathubodua?

Was it Bouvindâ? Nemetona? Senona?

Was it Sulis or Rosmerta?

Or even myself, Brixtâ, singer of spell-songs?

Taranis will never say.

Against Brigantiâ, any trick is only half a trick,

and any bind is only half a bind,

and any curse is only half a curse."

Hymn to Celestial Brigantia

Written by Nico Solheim-Davidson

The Celestial One
Enthroned On High
Who embodies the Heavens
Crowned with the moon above

Queen of the Heavens
Enthroned On High
Who tames wrathful thunder
Ordained by the rising sun

O Celestial Brigantia
Enthroned On High
You are the cosmos, far and near
And to you, I sing

Maponos

Written by Muriel Merser

I remember an age when there was no winter
when the sun never shrank from the world
nor grew to brutish power.

Our father was king in those days
he needed no weapon to rule
only the favour of Epona
who is Queen above all kings
and the caution of Cathubodua
who watches the skies
and the grace of Nantosuelta
of whom all beauty is but a reflection.

And you and I would watch Epona pull the sun
behind her golden chariot
as Sirona spun the silvery moon
this way and that in the starry firmament
and we would measure their movements
and we would tell stories of it
and put them in verse.

But even without the winter
our father's wheel spun steady
the mace forged of bronze
when I heard its' thundering song I knew
that it would be long indeed
before you and I could sing again
in praise of peaceful things.

Hymn to Tutela Brigantia Augusta

Written by Nico Solheim-Davidson

Exalted guardian
Who watches the north
With spear and shield in hand
I raise my cup to you

Great protectoress
Who stands over us
Within and outside of home
I greet you in kind

Awe-inspiring champion
Who remains firm
Against those who bring harm
I hail you with heart and soul

O August Brigantia
The stalwart walls of home
Who defends us from ill
I sing to you now

Cathubodua

Written by Muriel Merser

Colour of life, colour of pain
drips like wine from the swollen sun
as you raise my banner across heaven

time marches as the crow flies
memory is a two-way street
death from life, peace from pain,
love becomes blood becomes iron

fool is she who seeks prophecy
she makes victory hollow
and defeat inevitable

blessed is she who falls first in battle
never to know the fates of her sisters
who says "may" and never "will"
to meet the blade of Fortune fair and honest
to know Death only when she comes
that is the only glory.

Sixth Hymn to Brigantia

Written by Nico Solheim-Davidson

I sing to you, O Goddess Brigantia
She of the high places
Who was first into battle
With spear in hand

Watcher atop the cliffs
When the first winter came
Your spear raised for battle
And the giants you struck down

Protectoress of the Fort
The Pennines to the North
You carved and raised across the land
From the bones of slain giants

O Goddess Brigantia, enthroned high
Within the mountains you forged
Deep in the heart of the North
Hear me, as I sing now to you

Brixtâ

Written by Muriel Merser

You go before the sun
You follow the footsteps of the moon
Each morrow you do right by them,
But never by me.

It is you who wakes the summer
it is for you that she opens her splendid eye.
Your song is the song of the end of days
but you mourn a world that is not yet dead.

So I chain you, Brigantiâ,
with chains forged of the blood of your son
my curses cannot find you
but iron can bind flesh.

High above the wind and thunder
under stone let Grannus slumber
twilight skies and frost arraign thee
let Maponos seek, but vainly
let Taranis' hammer howl

through my cold sky strange and foul
silent be its smokeless burning
there beyond the autumn's turning
pale the sky's white mountains weeping
pale the ground, not dead but sleeping,
in your absence, rain and brightness
sickly over, sharp and sightless -
Fangs of winter, loose thy venom!
Scab the scars of scorching heaven!

Seventh Hymn to Brigantia

Written by Nico Solheim-Davidson

I sing now to Brigantia of the Rivers
Water-cloaked Queen, Divine Nymph
Who dwells within streams

With Derwent's water and a raven's song
With whispers of the sea and sparks of the sun
The voice of Maponos you restored

With these four ingredients
Mixed and brew within your cauldron
The first poet you created at summer's end

Your gift to Maponos, his voice returned
A gift to all of humankind and with it
I sing to you now, O Mighty Goddess

Epona

Written by Muriel Merser

Let Taranis have his thunder
if he doubts my discretion
let his fury light the path
no wings have I to melt
but hooves like meteors
I need only the wind.

Cast from the world of men, I ride
through the foulest fog of the starless sky
through the sea and the snow,
'neath the dead summer's eye,
through the depths of the night
where the serpent writhes

My hounds bay at Maponos' whistle
I am she who harbours the sleepless
who seek not rest but despise its theft
of that which the night once held from them
shining in the darkest hour

So which is the horse? And which is the rider?
And which is the giver of gold?
A star of three angles, like Hecate's torch
a needle lies red in the snow

I have known the disgrace
that love can make one suffer
you who are precious to me
I owe the chance
to fail as I failed
to triumph as I have triumphed.

Hymn to Brigantia of the Flames

Written by Nico Solheim-Davidson

O fierce Brigantia
Who lights and guards the flame
Of hearth, home, and fort
I sing unto you now

You were born of thunderous fury
That struck down the Three Tyrants
You first came into being
Formed where fire and water clashed

You spoke then to the world below
From the blazing flames
That sit upon the High Places
Your voice heard by all

You are the light which cleanses
And the light which forces back the darkness
The Tempered Fury and Eyes Upon The World
She who consumes that which is unclean

O Brigantia of Righteous Flames
You are the boundary betwixt chaos and order
Warrior of Lawful Destruction, Bringer of Renewal
I sing to you now O Fury of Taranos

Andraste

Written by Muriel Merser

Your grey eyes when the white mare came
unwavering vindicated
the sun sorrowed but you shone silver
(can a serpent laugh?)
No secrets with me, no debts,
we ride together!

a star of three angles
shines with dew
off the green rushes
and left askew
send me not hence
I bring no test
three nights we share
in frantic rest

You fought
no curse for an enemy?
Merciful prisoner
time demands sacrifice

Your brother earned his dance
all was fair in those days
summer ends
I can't tell if the crow is gloating or weeping

You lit this hearth I guard alone
no spear but the needle
am I
should have come with you

Your friends are many
I am the girl who held to you
through the winds that night
her hounds like sirens
the sea was a roiling cauldron

"The silv'ry mare needed no wheel
the river has one way to flow
so meet me, my love, at Midwinter,
our sorrow and I count the snow..."

The trees are no blind
when her eyes are the dust
we shelter with those
who have sheltered with us.

fidget by searching
a horn will call back to us
all heaven wanted you
quest not a prize

wandering static
restless high
as in the coals like dawn
my feet burn red
the ghost of your embrace

We share a name:
Victory
not Surrender

I left with you
I stayed for you
I do not seek to mourn the living

If you should return
I shall rejoice
If you should suffer
I shall avenge you
If you should die
I die with you.

Ninth Hymn To Brigantia

Written by Nico Solheim-Davidson

Brigantia, wise and creative one,
Goddess upon high and within rivers
Hear me now, as I sing unto you

Word and language you forged
From the breath and soul of man
So that we might speak and sing

Poetry you crafted within cauldron
From whispers of sea and Derwent's water
When the Great Son's voice, you healed

O Brigantia, goddess upon high
And goddess within rivers, hear me now
As I sing with the gifts you gave

Mnemosyne

Written by Muriel Merser

You know the path
to my house upon Olympus
you who tend the forges
of my daughters the Muses

It is said that your grey eyes
reflect a heart of cold steel

you, who shape beautiful things
from the molten metal
that fills my river in hell

You, who speak in honest terms
to gods and mortals alike
whose poems can burn the unjust
from the pages of good memory

Can the moon see its own reflection
in the murk of the Lethe?
Or is Her image too obscure,
lost to all memory but mine?

Hymn to Brigantia of Winter's Beck

Written by Nico Solheim-Davidson

Brigantia, Nymph and Goddess,
Who wields winterbourne beck,
To you I do sing now

Deep in winter's heart
The beck you raise up high
An aquatic shield across the land

You hold firm, you hold the line
Across Yorkshire and the Wolds
Above and below, you guard

Brigantia of the Winterbourne Beck
Shield-bearing Nymph and Goddess
In your brumal defiance, I sing to you now

Hera

Written by Muriel Merser

When shall we three meet again
upon the height of Nibheis-Beinn?
Not till the storm has come and passed,
and we shall see him strike his last.

We sought to claim the throne of heaven
two of the sky and one of the sea -
without the land, we were undone.
The stones were deaf to our betrayal.

Patience, patience.
The lightning strikes beneath the starless clouds,
the moon is hidden 'neath a tempest-shroud -
yet they were here before both storm and sea,
and every dawn predicts our victory.

Until then, we wait.
The ages will think us traitors -
but so long as we live
this battle is not lost.

Hymn to Brigantia Lugrînâ

Written by Nico Solheim-Davidson

Enthroned in night sky
Amongst a sea of burning stars
You show radiance from the heavens
With your bright, silver crown

River and ocean you bathe
In the splendour of your light
As across the dusky planes
Of the night, you ride

Brightly tressed Queen
Exalted beacon in the darkness
Who guides the hands
Of poet and artist alike

I sing of you now
Sweet voiced Brigantia
Highest of all divinity
Fairest lamp of blackened night

Sirona

Written by Muriel Merser

I coil and writhe about the world
one eye to the day and one to the night
when both are open
I can see both heaven and earth
But when both are closed
I can see nothing that is
but all that was
all that is known
all that is forgotten.

You will be free, Brigantiâ.
Your brother will seek you
Your lover will find you
Epona will tramp through a wall of fire
and the doors of the house of winter
shall be opened
and you will walk in the world once more.

Rejoice then with Andraste,
but think yourself not free.

The sun will wax

and become heavy with heat

the spear of Lugus will fell it

and Brixtâ will seek her prize

and you shall once again dust the pines

with deadly feathers from her pillows

and so it shall be

until the mace Maldnis is split

and Ogmios' chains are broken

and Lugus steps from his throne

and the last mortal king is unseated

and Epona shall reverse the blade of law

and the gates of Nantosuelta's realm shall be opened

and the Cathubodua shall rest

upon the shoulder of the world

.

About the Authors

Nico Solheim-Davidson

Nico Solheim-Davidson is a poet residing on the Yorkshire Coast. He is a Heathen with elements of Brittonic Polytheism in his practice. Nico is an avid lover of tea, symphonic metal, chip spice, and cats.

Nico was first published in Three Drops From A Cauldron's Samhain 2016 anthology, which featured his poem Samhuinn — Summer's End. Later that year, Nico self-published his first book, A Funeral In Erebus, which is composed of Nico's darker poetry.

Nico has also had poetry featured in other anthologies by Three Drops From A Cauldron, and has poetry featured in the Bardic Arts section of AlbionAndBeyond.com, a website and online resource for Brittonic polytheists.

Muriel Merser

Muriel Merser is a poet, playwright, and translator of French and German. She is a syncretic, matriarchal *bardâ* who takes as much inspiration from historical polytheistic practices as from modern occult traditions, always with a skeptical but interested eye pointed in the direction of neoplatonism and theurgy. For the sake of brevity, she usually just tells people that she's a witch. In 2023, she won the Toutâ Galation's Lîtus Maponî contest with her poem *Dâvnâ Îsarnî,* "The Song of Iron."

She currently resides in the alpine foothills of Styria, where she studies literature and involves herself in perhaps one too many theatrical and cinematic endeavours, both in English and in German.

Additional Resources about Brigantia

Brigantia: Goddess of the North by Sheena MacGarth (digital format only)

https://albionandbeyond.com/brigantia

Sacred Britannia: the gods and rituals of Roman Britain by Miranda Aldhouse-Green

Brigid Or Brigantia: A 'Pan-Celtic' Goddess in Profile by Charlotte Stone
https://repository.uwtsd.ac.uk/996/1/Charlotte%20Stone_Brigid%20or%20Brigantia.pdf

Other Books By Nico Solheim-Davidson

A Funeral In Erebus — First published 2016

She Set The Sky Ablaze — First published 2018

North Sea Rune Poems — First published 2022
 Also available digitally

Northumbrian Rune Poems — First published 2023
Also available digitally

Equinox — First published 2023
Digital only

Verses of the Nine Worlds — First published 2024
Also available digitally

Haiku Edda: The Mythic Edition — To Be Published

Printed and bound by CPI Group (UK) Ltd, Croydon, CR0 4YY

19/05/2025

01875969-0001